Angels and Fairies and Bright Rainbows

by Sara Lee Langsam

Illustrated by Madeleine Morin

A collection of poems dedicated to the eternal
child in each one's heart.

AMERISSIS PRESS

Langsam, Sara Lee
Angels and Fairies and Bright Rainbows
Amerissis Press, 2021
email: langsalight@gmail.com

Trade paperback: 978-0-578-94965-9

1. Poetry 2. Positive Concepts 3. Integrity 4. Good Values 5. Enlightenment

Text copyright © 1995 by Sara Lee Langsam

Illustrations by Madeleine Morin

All rights reserved. No part of this book may be used or reproduced by any means, graphic, electronic, or mechanical, including photocopying, recording, taping, or by any information storage retrieval system without the written permission of the author except in the case of brief quotations in an article or book review.

Printed in the United States of America

Table of Contents

To Mothers and Fathers 2
Night Frolic 4
The Fairies 6
The Water Sprites 8
Laughing Buddha 10
Spring 12
Song of Spring 14
My Friends The Trees 16
My Rainbow Kite 18
Clouds at Play 20
Hug the Sky 22
A Drop of Dew 24
Star of My Rainbow 26
Snow 28
The Little Snowflake 30
The Little Christmas Tree 32
Grandma's Woodburning Stove 34
My Special Friend 36
A Distant Star 38
I Am a Babe 40
A Six Year Old 42
Sir Galahad 44
A Special Kindness 46
Helping Hands 48
Marco Polo 50
Akbar Khan 52
I Am an Army Man 54
You Can If You Think You Can 56
America's Promise 58
Freedom's Song 60
The Poet and the Artist 62

Preface

Poetry is standing on a hill at sunset and seeing the clear, blue heavens flood with color — gold to deep orange to purple, fading to rosy pink' — the remnants of the last smile the sun shines upon the sky, the hills, the meadows and the seas before she bids them farewell.

Dedication

This book of poems is dedicated to my Mentor of the Spirit, Henry Wadsworth Longfellow.

A special thank you to Joyce Anderson and to Robert Mongrande for their assistance and encouragement.

To Mothers and Fathers

If your children you would see
Lie down to sleep peacefully
Take this little book of poems
And read them one, or two, or three.

Soon their little eyes will close
As they dream of bright rainbows
Of fairies and angels and flowers and trees
And the delicate scent of the warm summer breeze.

Night Frolic

Each night I lie asleep in bed
While dreams of beauty fill my head.
Angels and fairies beckon me
To join them in a night of glee.

With fairy wands they tickle my nose
As up the golden stairs they go.
A spiral of golden starry light
Leading to a rainbow bright.

0 my little friends, wait for me.
I long to join you, can't you see?
Together let us frolic and play
Until the dawn of a bright new day.

The Fairies

0 look, a fairy is in the grass!
Shhh! Don't speak or she'll fly away.
She raises her wand and touches a rose.
Come, let's ask her if she'd like to play.

"You can hold my fairy wand
And bless each flower in the glen.
Then come with me to my fairies' abode
Where we welcome all children.

"Children who believe in fairies.
In leprechauns and other dignitaries
Are treated very courteously
And given raisins and licorice tea."

The Water Sprites

My friends, the water sprites
Are a quick and nifty folk.
To watch them is a pleasure
For the joy that they invoke.

When the golden sun is shining bright
Upon the glens and nooks.
It's the water sprites that you will find
Dancing in the brooks.

Dancing and playing merrily
Leaping high and low
Their silken hair riding the breeze
Blowing to and fro.

Little Bubbles with her curly hair
Glimmering in the sun
Shaking her head with laughter
Her eyes sparkling with fun.

Sunshine standing in the brook
Striking a fancy pose
Shaking her pony tail saucily
Twitching her freckled nose.

Ah! My water sprites romping far
Leaping wild and free.
There aren't enough words in my heart
To tell what you mean to me.

Laughing Buddha

Fishes swimming in the stream
Golden fins all agleam
Swimming in the water blue
So crystal clear, they can see you.

O it's peek-a-Buddha, peek-a-Buddha, peek-a-Buddha, boo!
Yes, it's peek-a-Buddha, peek-a-Buddha, peek-a-Buddha, boo!

Laughing Buddha, eyes so bright
Big fat belly - pure delight.
Elves and fairies and children, too.
Let's see what Buddha has for you.

O it's peek-a-Buddha, peek-a-Buddha, peek-a-Buddha, boo!
Yes, it's peek-a-Buddha, peek-a-Buddha, peek-a-Budda, boo!

Buddha has a special pack.
It nestles snug upon his back.
And in his pack are wonders true.
All special gifts he has for you.

O it's peek-a-Buddha, peek-a-Buddha, peek-a-Buddha, boo!
Yes, it's peek-a-Buddha, peek-a-Buddha, peek-a-Buddha, boo!

If you are kind and good and sweet
And smile at everyone you meet.
If your friends are the flowers gay.
Why you will have a lovely day.

O it's peek-a-Buddha, peek-a-Buddha, peek-a-Buddha, boo!
Yes, it's peek-a-Buddha, peek-a-Buddha, peek-a-Buddha, boo!

All of Buddha's friends are here.
Forest folk from far and near.
Gnomes and leprechauns - their children, too.
Don't be shy; there's room for you.

O it's peek-a-Buddha, peek-a-Buddha, peek-a-Buddha, boo!
Yes, it's peek-a-Buddha, peek-a-Buddha, peek-a-Buddha, boo!

Spring

The sun shines bright.
The children play
In the golden light
Of a fine Spring day.

Song of Spring

A little bird perched on a branch
Warbled a song of spring.
The notes of joy - of life renewed
Caused my heart to sing.

My heart did sing, my thoughts took flight.
Into the air they flew.
Free to roam the whole wide world,
A wondrous scene to view.

A scene so bright, so crystal clear.
Where flowers of pastel hue
Shimmered and glistened in a radiant light
As they swayed to a fairy's tune.

The fairy played a hopeful song
To all on land and sea.
Now is the time to give to Life
The love God has given thee.

My Friends The Trees

I lie on the grass and gaze up on high.
My mother is earth, my father the sky.
The trees are my friends with their green leafy boughs.
The branches protect me from the cool, misty showers.

I hear the birds warble their song of good cheer.
They herald a new day, a day bright and clear,
A day when all on earth will join hands
And working together bring peace to the land.

My Rainbow Kite

I love to fly my rainbow kite
Of many-colored hue.
I long to fly into the air
The whole wide world to view.

Each color tells a wondrous tale
Of courage lost and found.
Of a child's trusting smile
That soothes a weary frown.

I'd like to share my rainbow
With the people that I meet.
And drop a tiny sparkling jewel
At each traveler's weary feet.

That he might pick it up and see
Its sparkling rays so bright.
Each ray of light a comfort
Will make everything all right.

Clouds At Play

The grass is green, the sky so blue.
I know just what I want to do.
I want to gaze into the sky
And watch the clouds as they go by.

Each cloud I see winks cheerfully.
As it glides by it waves to me.
Come up here, it seems to say.
What a lovely place to play.

Hug the Sky

When things go wrong and I want to cry.
When I feel sad and I close my eyes,
A little voice inside me sighs.
Stretch up high and hug the sky.

Hug the sky and feel the blue
Flow right down inside of you.
Feel the fluffy clouds so white
They tickle if you hold them tight.

When I'm mad and the sky looks grey.
When I want everyone to go away.
When Mother and Father and brother too
Don't please me no matter what they do,

I know that if I really try
And look straight up into the sky.
There is a secret part of me
That can make the anger go away.

If on my face I put a smile.
Why then after a little while
I won't have to pretend to be
I'll be happy — naturally.

Then I can go outside and play
And have myself a wonderful day.
The sun that shines so cheerfully
Is now shining inside of me.

A Drop of Dew

A drop of dew
Upon a leaf
Crystal clear
Upon dark green
Watery sign
Of new creation
Knight who heralds
A new born day

Star of My Rainbow

Star of my rainbow shining bright
Guide me as I sleep tonight.
Hold my hand and show me the way.
Tomorrow will be a wonderful day.

Snow

Snow
Falling softly
Upon a green field
Upon green grass
Covering each blade
A white carpet
Of velvety snow
A white field.

The Little Snowflake

I am a little snowflake
All pure and sparkling white.
No other snowflake is like me.
I dance on beams of light.

I kiss the silent treetops.
I cover the mountains tall.
The child who wakes from slumber
Sees a white blanket over all.

The Little Christmas Tree

I am a little Christmas tree
All green and sparkling gold.
And on the highest part of me
There sits a star so bold.

0 little star shine 'round the world.
Kiss every child so fair.
And when I see a face aglow.
I'll know that you've been there.

Grandma's Woodburning Stove

I like to sit on Grandma's couch
When frost is on the window pane,
And I am warm and snuggled down
And hear the patter of the rain.

I like to watch the fire dance
And see the flames leap all about
In Grandma's great woodburning stove
She never lets the fire go out.

Each flame takes on a graceful shape
As it moves quickly to and fro.
I hear the crackling sound it makes
As it jumps up, then falls down low.

I like to watch the fire blaze
And see the stove all filled with light
Until I yawn and fall asleep
To dream of flames all through the night.

My Special Friend

I have a friend who has a tie.
He has a twinkle in his eye.
With a smile he beckons me
To come and sit upon his knee.

I gaze into his tie and see
A whirling, spinning galaxy.
A galaxy of stars so bright.
Each star a whirling point of light.

I close my eyes and I can see
The stars all moving joyously.
They move across the vast, vast space.
I see a delicate pattern of lace.

O Milky Way, you are so grand!
I'm glad you are so close at hand.

A Distant Star

The night is dark, no moon is out.
The twinkling stars are all about.
I lay upon my bed and see
A distant star reach out to me.

The star is far away, yet near.
It seems to whisper in my ear
Of distant places that I might roam
To journey far away from home.

What is it like to live up high
In such a deep and endless sky?
Why not come and be with me?
We'll play together merrily.

Within my heart the star does say.
We must await another day.
You are a child of earth and sea.
For me the sky is my place to be.

I Am A Babe

I am a babe, so pure and good
In my mother's womb I lie.
So warm and snug and cozy
I full of joy abide.

My mother waits to welcome me
Into tender, loving arms.
And while she waits, I sleep and dream
Of other places and climes.

I travel 'round the world so wide
Full of hope and cheer.
Children with smiling faces
Before me do appear.

They tell me to be patient.
It won't be long for me.
Soon I'll come into the world.
My own true self to be.

A Six Year Old

A little girl of six years old
Is serious, yet sweet.
She knows the way things ought to be,
A room that's clean and neat.

Friends who laugh and play with you
And follow all the rules,
A six-year old knows what to do
And she will tell you too!

Sir Galahad

O it's Sir Galahad I'd love to be,
A knight of virtue and chivalry,
A noble heart and a courageous mind,
'Twould be difficult a finer knight to find.

O brave knight, you inspire me
To search the world for Truth and Gallantry.
And whene'er a brave and kind deed I do.
Then do I follow in your footsteps true.

A Special Kindness

Upon the road the man did lie
His eyes were closed, his breathing weak.
It was not known the reason why
He lay forlorn and could not speak.

A helping hand would meet his need
To raise him up, to bring him care.
A tender heart to succor him
Till strength returned and he could share

The story of his sorry plight
Of how and why on him befell
The dreadful woe which caused the fright
And laid him low, this would he tell.

A child passed by in youthful cheer,
A joyful song upon his lips.
Upon his face a frown appeared
As he beheld the man bereft.

He could have gone along his way
With no more than a fleeting thought
Of pity for the stranger's fate
And sorrow for what life had wrought.

The spark of love in him did live
Of mercy for his fellow man.
Who knows but what we freely give
Will return in Life's great plan.

The child did stop and bending low
He laid his head upon his breast.
He soothed the man as best he could.
Gave comfort that the man might rest.

He then went off to search for help.
Who would meet the stranger's plea?
The God who dwells in every man
Is there to help both you and me.

An act in loving kindness done
Is sure to reap a bright reward.
The joy we share with everyone
Will soon return to our own door.

Helping Hands

As I gaze around the earth, I see
The delicate flowers, the stately trees.
As I gratefully view the majestic land,
I am aware of "helping hands".

Hands unseen, hearts of love.
The gentle wafting breeze above.
All help to convey the design so grand.
All help to inspire us to share in the plan.

Every child who gazes on high.
Who watches the twinkling stars in the sky.
Knows in his heart that we are all one.
Each a thread in a tapestry spun.

Marco Polo

Marco Polo, Kublai Khan
The world expands for every man.
Behold the great explorer seeks.
His vision does the ages span.

New ideas, new ways to live.
With good will all cultures thrive.
The seed of hope which Marco brought
Until this hour does survive.

Kublai was the driving force
To see a world in harmony.
Marco Polo was the source
By which his vision could decree

A world where new ideas would gain
A foothold, taking root in earth
Made fertile as a vast terrain
From which the world achieved rebirth.

Thus does the great explorer prove
His faith in heaven's mighty power.
With God he seals his destiny
To place his stone in Life's great tower.

Akbar Khan–Akbar the Great

Let us the pages of history unfold
As we tread with footsteps sure
To peruse the greatness of scenes of old.
Stories of the days of yore.

Days when men of mighty deeds
Gave courage to the earth.
Men whose vision pierced the mist.
Whose hearts sought a true rebirth.

Such a one was Akbar Khan.
Akbar the Great was he.
Noble leader and statesman true.
He welcomed his destiny.

He reached for the light in the sun above
That shone o'er his wide domain.
And strove to anchor the light of the sun
In the hearts of his fellow men.

He knew that to follow the thread of Truth
One must the ages span;
That Truth is found in many creeds
And in the pure heart of man.

Each ray of Truth from the Central Sun
Sheds its radiance o'er the earth.
And finds a permanent abode
In the heart who knows its worth.

All who follow the ray of Truth,
From their hearts to the Central Sun,
Will find a wondrous story unfold,
A magnificent journey begun.

A journey which will never end
As long as life endures.
Truth leads us to heights unseen
And is the open door.

Thus did Akbar set his gaze
Upon a vision clear
Of life where Truth would reign supreme
And draw men ever near.

I Am An Army Man

I am an army man so tall.
I never feel afraid at all.
And when the enemy I see,
I challenge it with bravery.

I look it squarely in the face.
My bold look puts it in its place.

You have no power!
You can do no wrong!
I won't allow it! I am brave and strong!
I know from deep within my heart.
My courage fells you at the start.

You Can If You Think You Can

When treasured goal before you lies.
Not close enough, but yet not far.
When tender heart in longing cries.
And hands reach up to grasp the star.

Then must the will be firm and strong
To hold the vision of your goal.
And fear and doubt must be cast out.
It is your faith that makes you whole.

Yes, think upon your dearest wish.
Hold your desire firm in hand.
Then step by step pursue your dream
According to your mind's own plan.

For every dream that you hold dear.
And must of your life be a part.
Will surely manifest itself.
If you persist and not lose heart.

Thus strive and strive and don't give up
And you will surely reach the goal.
Reach up and seize the Victor's cup;
It is your faith that makes you whole.

America's Promise

We are children of many lands
Who have come to America's shore.
The torch held high in Liberty's hand
Has beckoned us and many more.

Freedom has a beautiful sound
To hearts that reach for the sky.
Freedom to create one's destiny,
To walk with one's head held high.

Freedom to choose one's way of life.
To strive to reach one's goal.
For this. Mother Liberty, we love you much.
And we call America home.

Freedom's Song

I run along the beach at dawn
As the sun begins to rise,
O sky, O sea, my heart beats free.
Sand and water greet my eyes.

The sun smiles down and warms my feet.
1 feel great joy in each heartbeat.
O sky, O sea, I long to be
Forever a part of eternity.

Biographies

Sara Lee Langsam taught high school Spanish and English as a Second Language in high school and elementary school. Words have always fascinated her and the beauty and meaning of life that can be captured in poetry.

Her books of poetry include *The Homeward Path* which includes both poems and essays, *The Voice of the Heart,* and *Angels and Fairies and Bright Rainbows.*

Sara Lee has also published a children's book–*Francis Bacon: Childhood Adventures* which includes *Francis Bacon: England's True Prince* and *Francis and Anthony: Inseparable Brothers.*

Her poems, essays, and children's stories portray on a subtle level the ideas and concepts she has learned in her lifetime of studying the world's many spiritual and religious traditions. The knowledge of these traditions and their role in our everyday life has given the author the opportunity through her books to share with others these vital life-enhancing concepts.

Madeleine Morin was originally from Michigan with a background in the secretarial field as an executive secretary at Ford Motor Company for the Staff Director of Public Relations in their International Operations.

After moving to Montana in 1984, her interests were directed to her real love of art work and calligraphy. For several years she worked with "The Old Christmas Barn" (a manufacturer of holiday and country collectibles) painting the smiling faces for their angels, santas, etc., assembling the baby angels, designing the signs used at their shows, and other art work.

She also created visual aids for private schools, greeting cards and illustrations for children's materials.

www.ingramcontent.com/pod-product-compliance
Lightning Source LLC
Chambersburg PA
CBHW060755090426
42736CB00002B/47